Worn Open Places

Worn Open Places

Poems by

Craig Nielson

© 2025 Craig Nielson. All rights reserved.
This material may not be reproduced in any form, published,
reprinted, recorded, performed, broadcast,
rewritten, or redistributed without
the explicit permission of Craig Nielson.
All such actions are strictly prohibited by law.

Cover design by Shay Culligan
Cover photo by Craig Nielson
Author photo by Craig Nielson

ISBN: 978-1-63980-726-0

Kelsay Books
502 South 1040 East, A-119
American Fork, Utah 84003
Kelsaybooks.com

for Laurie James and Chris Ransick

Acknowledgments

Thank you to the following publications, in which versions of these poems previously appeared:

Colorado Central Magazine: "Gift at Forty-Five," "What I Know So Far"
A Democracy of Poets: "Come Back to Us Everett Ruess," "Botanical Praise," "Birthday on the Fremont"
On Stage: River City Nomads: "Old Woman in the Supermarket"

Contents

I. what is lost

Every Heart	17
Dead Man's Curve	20
Gate B-25	22
Old Man Penman	24
Everything Will Be OK	26
Old Woman in the Supermarket	27
Unfriending the Dead	29
Ricky and Lisa	31
Night	34
Lessons on Drunk Driving from the Utah Highway Patrol	35
Come Back to Us Everett Ruess	37
Missing Climber on Mount Harvard	38

II. what is left

Gift at Forty-Five	43
Keep the Lonely Places Lonely	44
Cold Mountain Driving	46
New Mexico Farm	47
What More Can I Tell You About a Winter Day	48
Avenging the Cat	50
What My Father Said	51
Rogue River Ramble	52
Six Observations on a Spring Afternoon	55
Raven Heart	56
Birthday on the Fremont	59
Perception	61

III. what is wild

Escalante Still	65
Three Ways to Know the Desert	66
Botanical Praise	67
Trees Speaking of Spring and Other Matters	68
The Tall Grass	70
Flat Tops Promise	71
October, Colorado Trail	72
Winter Geese	73
What the Cat Tried to Tell You	75
Wilderness, a Conversation	76
Unknowable	78
Three Days in Zion with Walt Whitman	80

IV. what is essential

Preposition Place	85
Her Grandfather's Plan	86
Cessna Bioregionalism	87
Grandfather Carried His Name to America	88
Learning to Be Human	92
Boundless	93
As River, as Love	95
Garden Manager	97
Fruita Thanksgiving	99
Amity	101
Andean Ascents, a Love Story	102
What I Know So Far	107
Notes	111

Oh, it's a messed-up world, but I love it, anyway.

—Greg Brown

I. what is lost

Every Heart

San Francisco, December 2005

If every heart is one,
I am thinking that
I am not alone,
walking the steep hills

in this city of endless sidewalks,
and I recall that the poet's job
is to witness everything.
Like the holiday tree in Union Square

that casts its light upward,
the dark sedans brushing the night air
and the well-dressed,
filling the shiny stores like a reservoir.

And I am thinking that desire—
or should I call it envy?—
is like illusion
or some other simile,

like the truth about Venus
or absence before it is noticed,
or a simile for another city,
like the angry edge of North Beach,

or the upstairs room in the poet's bookstore
where even poetry becomes
a metaphor for what could have been.
Or like the narrow ribbon of Chinatown

with rows of vegetables and painted resin,
or the restless faces resembling despair—
or should I call it wanting?—
that remind me that poverty

is the great divider.
Or the many bodies sleeping in doorways,
and I am thinking
that the back side of every heart is longing,

and that perhaps my ten dollars
tucked under his water bottle
is equal to a prayer,
or maybe a ransom

for a lousy cup of coffee,
or levity from the cold ground.
Or that tonight I can hear a homeless man moaning
from some alley between the wired rooftops

Call an ambulance, I'm hurt, call a goddamned ambulance.
And I know he is homeless from the want in his voice
and because supplication is the sound of denial
when daylight wanes

into what we know as comfort,
where inside this yellow hotel room
I am trying to be thankful
for this small radiator and dry bed,

hoping that it might be something
resembling gratitude or a way to feel grounded
to something warmer
than the concrete outside.

And I am thinking that other cities
reside within every city,
that another America
is the same America we forgot to rename.

Dead Man's Curve

He was on the highway
on his back on the warming asphalt
his round-white belly
shining up to the sky
like a dead-eyed moon.

I saw the tightness of the curve,
the engineer's calculation of speed, radius,
the angle of the bank,
the fragmented glass and shattered plastic
and body fluids staining the road

like a dark and final mark on the earth.
And the part of me
afraid to be alive was saying no, no . . .
this is just not right
to die here on the pavement

next to the mangled machine,
a stranger administering
the chest compressions
a rancher directing the oncoming traffic
sirens down canyon growing louder,

the benevolent heavens turning above.
Or how we name these places of passing
"dead-man's curve" or "mis-calculation corner."
How the metal of the guardrail
remembers the over-corrections.

How a cliff face will always be
a cliff face, minus a few shards.
And how a body will always be
a soft thing in a hard world
or how another roadside cross

seems a noble but feeble gesture
for the wheel-bearing national memorial
that keeps rolling on forever.
And how not looking at the carnage
is impossible,

like how long it takes to get
an ambulance from Cañon City.
Or how reverence is automatic
as I drive slowly by
knowing, with a simple glance,

the difference between
a still-living body and a corpse.

Gate B-25

Our final night sleeping
with his familiar scent and
the closeness between us
the predawn rising
and brushing of teeth
then the river of cars racing east
across the buried prairie
toward the canopied carbon-complex
through the rote tyranny
of uniformed officials
to the shuffle line and moving sidewalks
the final stoic embrace at the gate
then he, heading down the carpeted ramp
pulling his small rolling luggage
disappearing around the bend.

Hopeless to glimpse him again in seat F9
as the moving-vapor, metallic fuselage
with rows of too-small windows
pulls away from the terminal
the dumb, still mountains beyond
and above, bunched clouds and a pale sky
streaming westward over the Divide
the half-continent beyond
and the vast Pacific beyond that.

My son hurtling away from me,
seated behind the plate glass,
wet-eyed
blank
staring
at the empty tarmac
the horizon of nothing
then willing a masked acceptance
and numbly rejoining
the terminal stream
crowded with strangers.

Old Man Penman

Old Man Penman was a cheap son-of-a-bitch,
which is probably how he ended up a millionaire.
He owned a burgeoning playground-equipment company in Utah,
a state that has more kids than Kentucky has ticks.

In '78, me, and my older brother, an arachnophobe,
worked for Old Man Penman three summers in a row
for 50 cents an hour.

His sweet wife paid us with crisp one-dollar bills
like they were printed in a basement.
Even before we really knew what getting boned was,
we figured out our hard toil was ill rewarded.

We spent long days straightening rusty sixpenny nails
and stacking spider-infested lumber
into huge piles next to the river,
my brother cringing with every new nest.

Our young bodies grew strong and tough,
our hands callused far beyond our age
but we knew then we didn't want to end up
like Old Man Penman, shuffling about the yard
in his greasy overalls, his knotted hands clutching
pipe wrenches like he was born with one.

Back home one summer, on break from college,
years after his passing, the new owners set the huge junk pile
ablaze, the harsh black smoke rising in the canyon
like a dark omen.

I wasn't going to miss that creosote-soaked junkyard,
and those long hours of hard labor and shitty pay,
but as the smoke cloud drifted west toward the city,
I somehow knew Penman and his spendthrift ways
were becoming lost to something new
and even scarier than those damn spiders.

Everything Will Be OK

for Laurie

Before your final stanza,
you wrote, "Everything will be OK
when you are OK with everything
disappearing."

More and more Ma-T
things are fading away,
but you and I have a history of losing
and finding things in this world.

I remember the waning light
high on the mountain as you joined
me across the veil to climb
and converse together

while recalling what was.
We carried our liminal exchange
as I guided you to the summit
and down the far ridge into the darkening forest.

How is it, Ma-T, that what we cling to most
is what leaves us too soon and how
needing anything is a setup for loss,
knowing everything eventually disappears?

Old Woman in the Supermarket

It might have been because I was blocking
her access to the cottage cheese that made her
comment on the time when she remembered
only one brand, and me, then remarking
on the superfluous varieties of cottage cheese.

Her one good eye pierced me like a hawk,
the other eye, crazy and casting a nostalgic
stare off into a distant, Depression-era remembrance.
"Look at all this damn food around here," she said.

Back in Denver during the worst of the years,
she told me about the hobo tents pitched along the Platte River,
her mother weeping quietly in the darkness of the room,
her childhood friends thinking they were rich because her
daddy had a government job and could afford to buy food.

"People starved back then," she said, her wild eye shifting
in waves as if running toward something.
"It lasted ten hard years until they started the war.
That's what saved us, the damn war."
"It's an interesting time to be alive," I commented.

"No, it's not," she quickly said. "It's an awful time to be alive.
The damn banks, they messed it all up, we'll all be
speaking Chinese.

We don't make a damn thing anymore."
She told me about the textile mills in the city and how she
would watch the patterns of the fabric emerge with each sweep
of the loom and how the act of making things made her proud.

"The '50s," she said, "that was the time to be alive,
everyone had jobs then and we all had something
new we could buy and money to buy it with. We don't even have
real money anymore, damn coins are sandwiched together
with tin."

In Sacramento, Tent City was more like a village carved out
of the strip of no-man's-land bordering the river and north
of the Blue Diamond Nut Factory.

All that food and water in one place with so much lack.
The tent-strewn underpass merging onto the great
boulevard loaded with strip malls and neon to the far horizon.

Unfriending the Dead

by 2070 more than half the people on Facebook will actually be dead

I started unfriending dead people.
I felt bad doing it, I admit,
but I figured they probably wouldn't mind
me cleaning up this small loose end.

Occasionally during an afternoon scroll,
I would see their smiling faces in my feed.
It's Steve's birthday. I should reach out,
make uncommitted plans to grab some coffee.

Then realizing they have left the social-media community,
their profiles and content uploaded to a new platform,
an even larger and more optimized marketplace.
I wonder how they would feel existing in the

numerical graveyard, a distant server
holding their thoughts and memories,
a cyber-ghost leaving their footprints
at the boundary of the living world.

But considering there are 107 billion dead
and 7 billion living (15 dead for every living),
I think of the social reach one could have beyond the curtain.
An ethereal algorithm of endless clicks and likes.

And so, with our modern, on-line lives,
with our hundred accounts and passwords,
houses full of broken electronics,
and the mess we all leave behind,

we ponder the likes and loves of our latest post,
the ads in our news feed we can't ignore,
our 400 friends we don't really know,
and the next Facebook event that will finally fix our lives.

We wonder how long it will be
before we too are posthumously unfriended,
joining the social community of the digital dead
to haunt our friends and family forever.

Ricky and Lisa

At the bus stop in winter
the bigger kids would punch Tony
hard in the shoulder
and then tease him about the scarred lip
he got from biting into a live toaster cord.

We would sit in the hard-chaired desks
legs stuffed between the metal rails
the smell of freshly peeled pencils,
secret notes and Cracker Jack toys
hidden under the hinged top.

When Lisa peed on the linoleum floor
a breath of silence was followed
by a roar of laughter.
Lisa died a little that day—
even at age seven I wanted to hold her.
The teacher tried to tell us about childhood diabetes
but all we could do was hope like hell it wasn't contagious.

My best friend Ricky was a tough kid
with a big grin who could not spell his last name.
I secretly fixed it for him on all his school papers.
What Ricky lacked in book-brained knowing
he made up for in gutsy forwardness
and enthusiasm for trouble.

Once we stole his big brother's Marlboro Reds,
smoked the whole damn pack on the trampoline,
jumped and flipped and wrestled and puked
our guts out over the frame and then passed out cold.

His mother found us later, sunburned and dizzy,
and coaxed us into the house with meat-and-potato stew,
the same pot of stew that seemed to be on the family
stove every day for ten years.

When we got too wet sliding down the hill at recess
the teacher made us strip bare and pick out girl's coats
from the rack; me in a puffed synthetic down with baby-blue
frilly trim with my naked legs sticking out.
Ricky got a nice little pink number with a faux fur hood.

As we sat in shock, staring at each other
from opposite sides of the classroom,
out of the corner of my eye,
there was pretty Lisa crying softly.
It was her coat I was wearing.
Lisa died a little more that day
and all Ricky could do was
grin that big goddamn grin of his.

Everything changed that spring afternoon on the bus
when Ricky pushed one of the Beerman brothers too far.
I remember seeing him jammed into the gap
between seat and seat back, his nose bloodied
and Beerman on top pummeling his jaw into the hard rubber mat.
Ricky ate more than his pride that day and for the first time,
I tasted fear.

Nobody messed with Beerman after that
and Ricky suddenly seemed not so tough anymore.
Years later I would visit Ricky,
all muscled and wild-haired,
installing a sprinkler system at his new house,
just 40 feet from the rusted trampoline frame.

Lisa grew up beautiful but died for real at age twenty.
Now, when I smell a freshly peeled pencil,
I can see her red cheeks and those big teary eyes,
and Ricky grinning like he'd done it all.

Night

night
gray and muted
in layers of mist and shadow

wall of rock
blocking
the edge of sky

landscape of improbability
informing the mystery
that caries us

day to day
scene to sorrow
to be alive

in the beauty
folds of earth
holding it all

remembrance
for the living
and the other

washed down
by rainfall
earth

witness
to the record
of time

Lessons on Drunk Driving from the Utah Highway Patrol

I was hard on Dad and his vehicles.

Note to all fathers: Never leave the keys to your fully restored 1965 Mustang convertible, with a 285 straight-six, lying around when you decide to go out of town with your mistress, leaving your troubled teenage son alone in the house.

I remember blasting up Interstate 15, headed to Evanston for 6.0 beer, the top down with Led Zeppelin blaring from the 8-track, half-drunk buddies piled in the back seat, and my best friend Ricky riding shotgun and dragging on a Camel. Driving drunk in 1983 was not only common practice, it was a recreational sport. Our biggest fear in those days was getting pulled over and having some asshole county sheriff make us pour out every one of our Coors tall boys into the barrow pit.

Christ, we thought we were so cool. Stupid little punks, we just wanted to get a good buzz on, score some ditch weed, and try to land the drunkest willing girl at the party. We never thought about consequences, we were young and would live forever if the beer kept flowing, and Wyoming kept its eighteen-year-old, legal-drinking age limit.

It must have been six months into my new drinking-and-driving career when Dad, in full Highway Patrol uniform, including his .38 Smith & Wesson double-action revolver, came up behind me at the dining table and dropped an 8½ x 11, black-and-white case-file photo right on top of my mashed potatoes.

Four drunk teenagers in a fast car had tried to outrun a freight train. They didn't quite make it and went under the steel-trussed boxcar at ninety-per. I'd never seen a human neck-stem before.

The impact had taken the front passenger's head clean off, while the driver's head was swung out wide, attached only by the left mandible. The kids in the back ended up somewhere on the far side of the tracks, unrecognizable. He dropped a second photo on the plate that told that story.

I hated my old man that night for showing me those pictures, but deep down inside I knew what he was trying to do. He was just another fumbling parent trying to save his kid.

Come Back to Us Everett Ruess

Everett,
wanderer of wilderness before wilderness,
seeker and maker of the inscrutable mystery
in the time before highways.
You and your burros,
probing those immeasurable broken canyons
and wrinkled mesas,
with your open, artist's heart.
Pack full of canvas and poems,
needless of anything more
than that kismet of wildness
under those yawning desert skies
rotten with light and stars.
Leaving us the way you did,
forsaken,
wanting you to remain missing
and never found.
Walking off with your fair smile,
filled, as you were,
with all that barren beauty,
into the red abyss.

Missing Climber on Mount Harvard

Gene, I don't know why I felt so allied to you when I found your summit note that day. There was a sorrow and confusion that led me to write down every word. I didn't know you were in trouble then, or maybe part of me did.

We could say I passed right by you on that final push along the other summit ridge, the sun diving down the back side of the sky. We could say my own fear that evening, the dread and uncertainty of the pinnacled summit with its precarious, hanging blocks and steep, exposed scree, was mixed up with yours. We could say I felt your presence but didn't really know you were there. I want you to know, Gene, I would have stayed to help had I found you, or maybe you never really wanted to be found.

If the sheriff had put down his coffee and ego long enough to consider all the information, if the forty SARS on the mountain looking for you had had the right beta, if you were not wearing dark blue against the dark rocks, maybe your office in Cleveland would not have to sit so empty, maybe your sister would not have had to board a plane. So many things could have happened differently, but let's face it, Gene, in your case a story full of speculation may never square against what is.

Gene, in the end it may not be up to us to know what the mountain will take or what the mountain will give. The summit rock is uncaring, it is not a place to linger too long. Like the stoic alpine goats who greeted me below the dimming summit, I suppose we all must learn when to climb and when to descend. But it goes to reason, Gene, that the better part of you has always been high on the mountain, maybe even high enough to have been waiting for the rest of you to return.

Tonight, the stars above my warm and sleepless bed are the same stars you might be looking at from your damp crevice. They are beautiful, Gene, and I know they will keep rotating from their center, that somehow it will all keep spinning with or without us, that even though I don't know how it all works, that it's all just a sort of turning. And somehow, I know you will come to understand the truth of this, like the genuine part of yourself, as you make your final climb home.

II. what is left

Gift at Forty-Five

And so it is
when the father is dead
when the last dog for twenty years is buried
when all the lovely women once cherished
are dispersed in the eight directions
and the barely detectable hum of bareness
permeates the rooms of the house
where sleep becomes an abstract idea
and the only avatar to appear
is the rail-thin visage of a cat
who, like you, has never taken on
the virtues of stick-to-itiveness
who with a wistful head
smelling of oiled alley discards
and a voice full of gravel and lent
enters the empty house like providence
gifting you with its ragged companionship
as you portion together
the inevitable slide to middle flesh
where likeness still attracts.

Keep the Lonely Places Lonely

The last billboard out of Santa Fe
suggests that Jesus may be calling
on my cell phone, asking if I will answer.
I steadied the wheel and hit the throttle,
dropping down the shoulder of Glorietta Mesa.

Past the piñon-juniper hillsides
of cliched adobe houses,
beyond the rolling gated ranches
and overgrazed rangelands
towards I-40.

Past the beat-up edge
of the Permian Basin south of Roswell.
Bleary-eyed apparitions of island ranges
appeared on the horizon,
gas flares and GPS-festooned, fleet pickups,

belly-loaders and dust plumes,
acrid air searing the soft membranes.
Onward through the Carlsbad wastelands,
the Guadalupes rising up like a cathedral.
By the time I crossed the Black River,

and entered the Chihuahuan desert,
I knew I was out there.
Twelve hundred miles of open, dry lowlands
and distant ranges filled the windshield.
The boarded-up gas station sign

told me to "keep the lonely places lonely."
So I kept rolling, past the peyote-inspired
art hanging in the Marfa galleries,
miles stacking on the ODO,
to the far tip of the great Southwest.

Then hours on foot
over shattered limestone
through the ocotillo and sotol slopes
to the apex of the Rio's Bend.
A place so far and lonely that even Jesus
would not be able to reach me.

Cold Mountain Driving

Driving off the cold mountain towards the town below,
the old pickup rocking on its stiff springs,

past the lonely cabins with their pale porch lights
and tendrils of early season smoke,

past the canyon's eerie moon-burnished ridge
with its oddly bent pines cloaked in mist,

beyond the wind-howled peaks
pulling on their first base layer of white,

toward the small shimmering grid where the last of the summer
tourists have returned to their bright cities,

teetering between the bonanza and the lull,
embracing the shoulder-season melancholy like a new occupation,

the locals reclaiming their rightful places at the taverns,
the town, the gleaming mountains behind,

surrendering to the loss of balmy weather dreams,
a reluctant dimming just before the pending dark.

New Mexico Farm

Toasting the tall summer harvest,
living that day was as good
as any to be remembered.
Eight months beyond

the deep winter loss
that blew through the sunflower stalks
and the open windows of the old pickup
like a rustling omen of family secrets

sent out on the wind.
How fitting the high sun
to obliterate that which no longer serves
the cycle of seasons or the memory of seeds.

To push forth from the warm soil
a bounty of life renewed
and for this, a toast to all that is good,
to all that lies beyond.

To the long-day light
flaming the worn hills
bracing the little farm
from the spinning world.

What More Can I Tell You About a Winter Day

What more can I tell you about a winter day
that you do not by now understand?
That the home we know
is still at hand,

disguised under a cover of new snow,
the familiar obscured
yet present.
That we can make out the contours,

the swells, the rises,
the heavy-limbed and silent trees,
the flash of paint in the winter birds.
That we, too, are blanketed

in recurring layers,
disguising our warmer selves,
adjusting to the thickness of things,
accepting the hush of it all,

the muffled mess of the world.
That the half-weight of a child's gloved hand
is a welcome heaviness
tugging at our limbs.

That the long nights
are terrible with stars and distance.
That during the witching hours
our dreams strike out on their own,

into the deep cold
in search for what lies beneath the snow and ice,
in search for what makes us not alone,
for the heat that has left the land.

Avenging the Cat

It may yet hold true
that death
comes in threes.
I had no plans to rejoin
the business of cats,

but when the last dog
followed my father to the grave,
we found ourselves at the shelter
signing forms for a huge tabby
and a lanky Russian blue.

Chattier than a Chekov monologue
and faithful as the old lab,
I grew close to that long, sleek Russian.
But when he disappeared one early August
afternoon, I knew I was in too deep.

I suspected the hand of the itinerant
neighbor who lived alone
with his brood of anger,
threatening the town deer and racing
his muscle car down the alley.

When the new cat, six months old,
failed to return from his evening hunt,
my dark fear turned to thoughts
of animal ways a man could meet his maker.
But alas, it takes time to plan a good murder.

What My Father Said

Son, true friends come in small numbers.
If you run out of fingers,
you counted wrong.

There will be those who use that word
as if it were a placeholder for some allegiance,
a space to fill, maybe used again,

then lost to the pile of failures,
or to the file labeled disappointment,
or whatever antonym you can think

of for "genuine." Son, the lucky man
will have a few of them and learns,
over time, how to separate

the bull-swingers from
the ones who show up,
the takers from the givers,

the joiners from the ones
who, with little to gain
or maybe, little to lose,

will engage you in a common pact,
unwritten and unspoken,
but understood.

Rogue River Ramble

for Chris

I asked my brother, a long-haul trucker,
what he thought of Oregon.
"It's just a shit-ton of people
living in the pine trees," he replied.

I thought of our ancestors
who followed the Oregon Trail west,
then headed south to Utah
at the fork in Wyoming.
Other over-landers headed
to the Rogue Valley to start farms and families.
What if my ancestors had taken that route?

Through the dullness of late fall,
I wend my way along the river,
the rounded mountains layer themselves
together in receding shades
of green and gray.

Sun-splashed hillsides
with wide-spaced black oaks in a shock of grass.
Farm after farm of possibilities.
Wild blackberries that can take over a place
and forests thicker than anything
in my arid homeland.

And the Rogue,
born on the slopes of a blown-out volcano,
flows west, free, and wild to the sea.

It gets a man thinking about independence and greenery . . .
Dammit, you can grow things here!
which is what brought the over-landers in the first place.

And that Ashland town, what a charmer.
Go ahead, buy up a clapboard cottage
with a wrought-iron fence.
Fill up your cup with a steamy latte
or a lavender-infused kombucha.

Throw a few crumbs at the ducks
in the pond by the Shakespeare theater.
No matter how you groove,
this town has your sweet spot.

But even good towns have their dark side:
At Jackson Wellspring,
the clothing-optional hot spring
on the rough edge of Ashland,
a less charming scene unfolds:
a young drifter guts out
a Gregorian chant from the shower,
while an old drifter dries his wrinkled body
in front of the mirror.

At the campground,
I give five dollars
to a down-and-out couple:
bus fare so they can make
the morning shift on the hemp farm.
Oregon gig economy, I suppose.

As they walk away, it all just makes me wonder
how human habitat might be part of our DNA.
That the place we inhabit is the same place
we hold in the landscape of our mind.
That place matters and where we belong
is a place where we can thrive.

A good poet friend moved here from Colorado
to care for his sick wife,
then got sick himself and died.
Maybe it had nothing to do with the place,
but I knew he struggled to make it feel like home.

And how many homeless hippies dressed
like wizards does it take to change a place like this?
How many wealthy Californians does it take
to fornicate all the good towns?

And what happens here when the big fires come?
Hemp burns just as easy as any tree
and maybe the shit-ton of people living in the pine trees
will need a Plan B.

But in the end, none of it really matters,
maybe our task is to make home wherever we are,
maybe we need to plant more trees, and maybe,
we all just need more wizards.

Six Observations on a Spring Afternoon

1. Optimism is proportional to day length.

2. Harley Davidsons are the harbingers of better weather,
   birdsong and insect wings be damned.

3. Cottonwoods spewing their seeds to the wind
   like a dreamy orgasm of April snow,
   become a respiratory hazard.

4. That coming out of winter,
   all of us are the walking wounded,
   our seasonal losses the small wrinkles
   at the corners of our eyes.

5. That the loveliness of a spring afternoon
   draws us into the secret heart of nature
   where the siren song of the universe
   untethers us from the world
   we thought we needed.

6. That cats are the earth's solar masters,
   always finding the light and heat
   and proving once and for all
   their preeminence over dogs
   who, while barking incessantly
   on a spring afternoon, are twice
   as maddening as the same damn dogs
   barking on a grey January day.

Raven Heart

Raven heart beats
above the sunbaked canyons and arroyos,
over reservation wastelands,
hogans built before driveways
standing alone in the desert,
over the muddy, serpentine rivers,
the sun-damaged rows
of government housing,
the liquor stores of capitalism,
over the last fifty Mexican grey wolves
in a desert island range.

Raven heart beats
over the monolith of Shiprock,
the forested plateaus
of the Apache reservation,
the tidy neighborhoods
and strip malls of Tucson,
the saguaro and ocotillo desert beyond.

Raven heart glides
in the carbon-filled skies
over Gallup, New Mexico,
where inebriated men
in Levi's and long-sleeved,
rhinestone-cowboy shirts
beg for change at the Shell gas station
near the on-ramp to Interstate 40.

Raven heart soars
over the home of a mother
in Prescott, Arizona,
where family and friends gather
among boulders to discuss rain gutters
and rooting javelina that raid her night garden.

Over Sedona, where it costs ten dollars
to see Oak Creek and the red-rock river crossing,
where the majestic cypress trees
display their improbable peeling bark,
the color of desert spring.

Raven heart glides and dives
over the crowded Safeway parking lot
in Flagstaff, Arizona, on Easter Sunday,
where a single mother loads plastic bags
of groceries and a baby
into a rusted minivan full of children,
abandons her shopping cart
and pulls away with a bad muffler
and squealing power-steering pump.

Raven heart flies over a Navajo boy
in a hooded sweatshirt walking
against the wind along the narrow
shoulder of U.S. Highway 163
in Monument Valley, past bony
reservation ponies under a coal-dust sky.

Raven heart beats in a man
traveling east on U.S. Highway 160
in an air-conditioned Honda looking for his
peace-sign ball cap lost in the wind
outside Tuba City.

Raven heart beats in a couple looking
for a heart-shaped rock among the ordinary rocks
lining the walkways of a closed coffeehouse
in Bluff, Utah.

Over a torn flag missing all its stripes,
whipping on the side of the road
outside Mexican Hat near the San Juan River bridge,
over the scarred land
and still-wild geography below.

Raven heart stitches the wonder of the western
interior into a collage of road and memory,
offering its sarcastic corvine cry
to a staggering man on a dirt road,
in a treeless city on the edge of the reservation,
who sees peace rolling across the desert
like a tumbleweed, coming to rest at his feet,
where he picks it up, dusts it off,
tries it on for size, and smiles.

Birthday on the Fremont

Birthday on the Fremont—
fifty years riding the big orb
around the sun.
It's warm in the desert,

the muddy river
murmuring its gravity song.
It's good to sink
your feet into the sand,

to sit amid the strata of rock,
to witness the river's passing
and the breeze cuing
the yellow cottonwoods.

It takes more than a day
to reconcile a life
but a day is more than enough time
to find the stillness.

Come evening, I loose the dogs
for a final swim down the river,
their powdered carbon
suspended above the ripples

like some holy shroud,
ashes to ashes, dogs to dust.
After the final light
fades from the canyon,

it's time to rise from the bank
and welcome the fire's heat.
After a passage in the mystery
it's good to grab on for another turn.

Perception

Desert night
sky
looking up
at the big
out there
it feels mighty good
to be grounded
to this old
earth.

III. what is wild

Escalante Still

I could say that dusk in the canyon
was perfect as any common
evening, that the sun's last rays had
reddened the cliffs even more,
that the cottonwoods below
were a cloth of green and yellow
radiance, that the closing light winked
below the notch of the rim, that the
stillness of my camp beneath the
rampart was a holy and peaceful
moment, my back against the warm rock,
the river humming its absconding song,
the nightfall bats squeaking overhead.

Three Ways to Know the Desert

1. There! Gambel oak and box elder, there,
   the stream-bank willow, there, the carcass of
   ponderosa, half-buried in the sand. Grow too
   close to the river and the floods will get you. But
   for some, getting your feet wet is a necessity for
   which there is only one other option, the tamarisk
   and Russian olives having their way with the bank.

2. Walking on sand will teach you tolerance,
   the sink and the push, the quarter-slide back,
   and to an ant, a square meter of sand is an
   entire desert, a habitat of small needs, every
   ant a wonder not to be stepped on, nor the
   unwearied and gleaming darkling beetle dotting
   across the sand, big sagebrush perfuming the trail.

3. Letting it all rumble up and settle down, last night
   the wind, a howling and building force, the gesture
   of it bashing the high limbs of the cottonwoods,
   cloud anvils marching from the southwest, the
   cliff above camp halving the night sky, allowing
   glimpses of fine filigree stars arcing around Orion,
   snug in a face-open cocoon, a body bag for the living.

Botanical Praise

So, I asked the double jack pine snag
clinging to the side of the mountain,
great tree, were you the tree of knowledge?
All trees living or otherwise, replied the pine,
are trees of knowledge.

So, I asked the shrubs and bushes,
the colonies of shadows populating the land,
oh, shrubs and bushes, why do you grow so broad
and with such equability?
And they answered,
Something has to anchor this old earth.

So, I asked the perennials,
the boundless regenerators rising from
their matted death,
perennials, are you the harbingers of life?
And the perennials answered,
No, we just have to learn
when to lie low and when to rise.

So, I asked the multitude of annuals,
the great flourishing of color and fruit,
annuals, why must you blossom and produce
for such a short while?
And the annuals replied,
Impermanence is the nature of things.

So, I asked the weeds
proliferating by the thousands in my dry yard,
loathsome weeds, why can't we praise you
as we do the other plants?
Praise, said the weeds, *is for fools.*

Trees Speaking of Spring and Other Matters

Father ponderosa
your children are all here
on the pinwheeled edge
of your shadow.
You are the idea of creation
watching over town

from your station
on Methodist Mountain.
Can I say you are beautiful?
Brother cottonwood
with your broken crown
and sweetly furrowed arms

gesturing toward home ground
soon you will be a cross for the land
when the trains ran coal up the river
but still your old roots
will find a way
to awaken the residue

of the river learning the land
and your wistful
and shading crown
will turn its heady face
to the high-sun sky.
Can I call you promise?

Honest town
with your legacy of gables
and broken sidewalks
almost feels more ancient
than the mumbling river
with its song

of always leaving.
Wood smoke
made of vanilla
and some slippery
white-boned
part of the river

is trailing towards Orion
offering its carbon breath
to night air and a million tiny deaths,
and our own accumulation
born in the silent hours
of the fallow season of the heart.

But to deny roots
their dark and sinking destiny
is equal to shame
cast into the river
because we can never
fully love the land.

And we are left to sigh
and know that it is perhaps
the holy breath
rising from the fallible
and ever leaning
flesh of spring.

The Tall Grass

Evening solitude, a walk in the tall grass. Last light of day, the purple glow of clouds. I walk the tall grass, hoping to find a piece of myself. The cool, wet blades lick at my pants. The sounds of children laughing, the broken fence lines, dashing sparrows, their evening dance. The dog runs wild, hidden by the tall grass, cutting and arching, freedom in his blood. Something draws me, this field of tall grass, a holdout against the surrounding encroachment. Peaceful for now, the tall grass sways defiantly. Once more, I return to the other side.

Flat Tops Promise

I've seen your namesake massif
from Highway 131 headed to Steamboat,
your broad-banded cliffs and pocketed
alpine meadows, your tapestry
of green on green, and your great
flat block of basalt that beckons
the backcountry traveler.

I've seen your startled bucks
in October, when your aspen glades
coin the stiff air in breaths of orange
and yellow, your open, placid slopes
that draw me into your mystery of
wild yearning, and someday I promise
to ascend your flanks and stretch

out on your flat tops, end to end,
moving through your verdant wilderness,
among your one hundred and ten lakes,
my fly rod busy with your cold trout,
or in winter skinning your sun-burnished
shoulders to your broad back
then carving your face with S's.

October, Colorado Trail

Boot prints on a sunbaked path, softened by red-brown maple leaves, dried stems, and rotting twigs, spongy underfoot.

Trailside balsam root with curled leaves and drooping, pale-yellow heads hanging on withered stems. The sweet, flat smell of decay hangs in the air. The smell of soil being made.

An indigo sky dappled with cirrus, pierced by a brilliant orb slung lower in the south, teases about its warmth. Families of aspen changing in turn weave a textured mosaic of flaming colors, like wrinkled linen up and over the summit slope, their cake-white trunks grouped tightly with ragged charcoal knots resembling eyes.

Fir and spruce massed between in dark and darker shades as if suddenly they were greener. Meadow grasses gather afternoon light. Grama and bunchgrass burn radiant gold, as if the meadow itself were the light.

Gambel oak branches scratch the sky, oddly grey as if they'd never been that color. Grey as if they'd never been there. Above, a billion shimmering coins twist on flat-leaf stems, refracting light at a thousand different angles, their soft hypnotic rustling a portent of winter's steady approach.

Winter Geese

When I hear wild geese overhead
I stop what I am doing,
make my way outside
to an open view of sky,
gaze upward in wonder and listen.

I open my ears to their passage
reporting in the cold air.
I ponder the white hulls of their bellies,
plump loaves of winged bread.

I imagine their detached view
of the world passing below
their V-formation,
the currents of northern air
lifting their grey, Branta wings,
the strain of muscles in their
black, chin-strapped necks.

When I hear wild geese overhead,
I think about their purposeful destination,
like unionized, long-distance truckers
hauling their loads from Minnesota,
bypassing all the checkpoints
and weigh stations along the way.

Or like Winnebago snowbirds
heading south to crowded
RV parks in Arizona.

Or how in recent years
they appear conspicuously in winter,
circling the snowless landscape below,
staging their phantom migration
like bewildered climate refugees,
then returning to nearby golf courses,
parking lots, and fields,
scratching for forgotten grain.

I think about their interrupted
and shortened journeys,
like cheapskate tourists
staying closer to home
due to higher fuel prices,
and eating in roadside Mexican restaurants.

Or confused groups of old men
telling the same stories over morning coffee
then forgetting what they were supposed to do today.

When I hear wild geese overhead,
I think about warm southern latitudes I've never visited.
I imagine roofs made of feathers and clouded sky,
coats made of sleet and down,
and windows made of lost horizons and distance.

What the Cat Tried to Tell You

In the blackest hour
sleep hinging between
misery and enough,
a nocturnal messenger,
coat sleek and cold as a board,

will come in from stalking the dark
to walk across your blanketed crotch,
his tactile paws, heat-seeking probes,
his diamond head nudging your hip
as if to speak:

Rise
from your slumber
and hunt the night.
The solution you seek is out there,
awake among the shadows.

Wilderness, a Conversation

Wilderness,
few of us really know you,
being as you are,
the green and tan blanks on the map
the cartographers forgot,
the roadless places where ideas about wildness
seek a comfortable rest.
You are so easy to love from the living room couch.
It's so comfortable to pine for your divine splendor on PBS.

Wilderness,
your many chapels are far too quiet for most folks.
You offer your wind-song whispers and babbling streams,
and your monotonous forest sighs.
But even your resident ravens, with their croaking laments,
must consider your numerous occasions
to think, or to really listen.

Wilderness,
you are not the million-dollar RV view,
the national park drive-through
(though you do look splendid through the windshield).
You are not the John Muir wanna-be rambler,
the visitor center gift shop,
nor the glossy calendar on the kitchen wall,
the refrigerator magnet.

Wilderness,
you are my kind of danger
with your ankle-busting talus,
lightning storm retreats,
cougar tracks that circle back
and big bear bumps in the night.
I relish your opportunity for peril.

Wilderness, do us all a favor:
Bring back your large predators,
take one of us from time to time.
You have much to teach us about humility,
about needs versus wants,
about being one of your resident animals.

Wilderness,
make me labor for your summit pass,
I've never been afraid of hard work for you.
Burden me with what you've got,
take this big man down to your home ground.
I promise I won't stay long.
I'll move on once you've wildflowered my mind
and rivered my evenings with your endless stars.

Wilderness,
we all want a piece of you,
an emblem of your restoring expanse,
a taste of your wild freedom,
your backcountry in the back of our minds.

But, let's face it,
my kind has not been kind to you.
Before us, you were everywhere.
It is not you we should fear,
but we, the many, our needs
bigger than your resource.

Wilderness, keep your distance
until what grows in our hearts . . .
is larger than your open sky.

Unknowable

That the desert is unknowable
may guide our loneliness
through the broken red canyons.

Needless of longing, unlike
taverns that need dry mouths,
like prayers offered for thirst.

We throw our bodies soft
upon the rock, miles for millennium
rock answers back

Flesh is a flash
a short flood
on the long geologic line.

Perhaps our minds are better tools
to probe the vast regions
our hearts a better measure
of that which is immeasurable.

So let the desert birds
with their sweet songs of communion
keep the morning.

Let the white sun have the day
the wilderness of galaxies
the clear night.

So that we may know
the deeper slots
of our slender time.

Where our scoured pockets
may hold a small and vague
piece of the mystery.

Three Days in Zion with Walt Whitman

Far above the main canyon under the
first rays of sun, I loved myself as everyone.
What has found me over and over is what I seek,
this and the warmth of sun also are true.

Myself a gatherer of debitage, acquisitioner and
inventorian of resources discarded or otherwise.
Myself of the brown earth as everyone,
as common and uncommon as any man or woman.

Myself of war-proud father and curved-
bone shame. Myself of the underutilized
parchment, of backcountry persuasion
and front-country selectivity.

What warmth we gather, the earth will take
back. To comprehend these myriad canyons
is to abandon myself. The blue jay shrills
at the edge of the gash, the sound falling

into the canyon. The tug of so much
emptiness below the rim is an invitation,
and this also is true. The earth opens
herself, revealing the flesh of her mantle.

I am the anatomist arriving too late,
the rock is continuously slumbering
but, like all dreamers, shifts and rumbles
do occur and only the sunlight makes it so.

At times like this geology fails me
in favor of wonderment.
Uplift and erosion
uplift and erosion

chant it like a creation song,
uplift and erosion, the heave, the thrust,
the unknowable shadow in the slot,
the amorphous core,

antediluvian and primordial,
the warp and weft,
the open earth,
here, here.

In the depths, I hear the crickets calling
under the high sun, but who am I to
question their timing? Of the multitudes
of plants that grow here,

I have come to know several well.
I can tell you about the majestic ponderosa
knuckled to the rock,
the burning maples holding

the color of last fall,
the Scarlet Gilia willing
itself through the seasons.
That all living things are vessels,

myself as everyone, also the same,
some days holding more than others.
That all of it is good, considering entropy
and the cycle of things.

That such fecundity exists is a miracle,
that all are lovely and deserving.

Fecund, Canyon Wren, songbird of lament
Fecund, plateau grasses, gentle sway
Fecund, fellow man, though many:
mapmaker, name-giver of place
trail-builder, path-carver of cliff face
backcountry ranger (your job is sacred if any job can be)

Fecund, white-sneakered tourist
you are every bit as deserving as I and everyone
Fecund, loud child, shattering the silence of the canyon,
you will remember and love this place.

But higher in the canyon
there may be rules regarding silence.
And now, the sun is being
swallowed by the western wall.

That it will return is a miracle
for which we are equally worthy.
For now, it is enough
to sing the song of all wild places,

to sing the song of this place,
the song of the West,
song of myself,
song of everything.

IV. what is essential

Preposition Place

Head over the Great Divide
under a September sky
beyond the San Juans

wearing their first winter jacket.
Keep going past Danish Flat
across the Dirty Devil

following the two-lane
beneath the high nipple
of the Henries.

By now, you are beyond
Caineville Wash,
near the edge of it all.

Keep driving west
among the Bentonite Hills
toward the far horizon

until red fills your windshield.
Go ahead, cross Carcass Creek,
the big pines

will be waiting
on the other side.
But between you and me

the place
I really want
to be

is just up ahead
over the mountain
around the next bend.

Her Grandfather's Plan

for Janine

At her grandfather's cabin in Garfield
standing together on the southern deck
in the April evening light
our bodies apart but somehow touching
the beauty in her eyes seeing the beauty in mine
the sweep of our separate lives
joining like the two forks of the river
swelling with the flush of spring.

And again, on the flank of Bull Hill
far above the swollen currents of Lake Creek
we laid our bodies down
on the warm stone of Split Rock
as the hush of evening fell across the
forested basin.

How many heart-shaped rocks must one gather
to find the one that leads back home?
How many miles must one travel
to find that which takes a lifetime?

I placed my hand on her slender leg
her hand twining with mine
as the ground below fell away
leaving only sky above,
the stillness of the mountain air
and above that,
the final light on Ellingwood Ridge
shining upwards
like a golden arc.

Cessna Bioregionalism

My father, gone now many years, was a pilot. I grew up flying with him over the badlands of southern Utah. The map of my bioregion looked more like a satellite image of a dead camel than a sketch of the Emigration Canyon side roads of my neighborhood where I rode my bike and fished the creek.

All that fractured and heaved rock, burnt caramel and tawny-red, splayed out for hundreds of miles, viewed from the Plexiglas windows of the Cessna and burned into my memory like the desert sun scorching Zion below. We took off and landed in just about every small Mormon town on the Colorado Plateau from Blanding to Cedar Mesa, Moab to Escalante.

The first time I saw Rainbow Bridge was from sixty feet off the deck of Lake Powell, with a steep, hundred-mile-an-hour bank to the left so I'd get a better view. Dad often hinted at an earlier feat of flying a Super Cub under the bridge on a dare, but he was then quick to admonish me, using his favorite pilot proverb: "Son, there are old pilots and bold pilots, but no old, bold pilots."

I liked imagining him screaming off Navajo Mountain like a rockfall and then making that impossible box-canyon pull-up and carve to the northeast, the final and delicate tipping of the wings to clear the arched walls, then the mechanical rage of the propeller blasting back out over the water and scaring the living hell out of drunken houseboaters.

All these years later, the plateau weaves itself into my dreams where trembling cottonwoods—Fremont, not those narrow-leaf half-cousins along this Colorado River—and those sheer Navajo cliff faces, all varnished and buffed, draw me back home.

Grandfather Carried His Name to America

Names like rivers carve histories
away and toward home ground.

grandfather of the three islands
grandfather of the slight elevation

The coffeehouse in Copenhagen felt like a living room
what is familiar is often a compass.

Belonging to bedrock
surrounded by two oceans.

grandfather of wood grain and cobble
grandfather of wheat and linseed oil

They came looking for you and others
the promise of land and opportunity.

grandfather who followed God to America
grandfather waiting in Liverpool for his ship to come in

At Ellis Island the immigration officer hated Swedes.
To make it rougher on you he turned you into one,
taking your name's "e" and giving it an "o."

grandfather of the wide Atlantic
grandfather who traded sea breeze and his name for an idea

The rail line ended at Rock Island where the Oregon Trail began,
the gathering of Zion along the wide Mississippi.
They were your people now
and Iowa lay before them.

After crossing the Missouri,
they took to the north side of the Platte River
to avoid conflict with the overlanders.
Handcarts, wagons, and oxen.

grandfather of the great migration
grandfather who walked across a continent

In Nebraska, the prairie
is another ocean
with a different name,
fish are swimming beneath the grass.

grandfather of the Great Plains
grandfather of thunderstorms and thin leather

There are wagons at Scottsbluff
pointing westward.
A remnant of the trail
can be seen.

grandfather who never imagined the size of America
grandfather who had never seen mountains

In Guernsey, Wyoming, the ruts are still there
and the names of those who crossed
are suggestions in the soft sandstone.

grandfather of creaking ballads
grandfather of callused hands

There are countless graves marking the way,
there are many ways of passing.

grandfather of lean bones
grandfather who kept walking toward the promised land

In Utah, Brigham was starting a revolution
trees were planted in the desert
corn was wrested from the clay
the earth was made to yield a harvest
granite quarried in the canyons
firs felled from the forest.

grandfather in Wyoming stepping through the sage
grandfather of little water
grandfather dry as bread

South Pass is the great gift of the Rockies,
even mountains have ways of yielding.
Many gave up and settled
where they stopped walking.

grandfather of the homestretch
grandfather of the Bear River

At Little Mountain, outside of Salt Lake,
a loaded handcart was flung off the mountainside.
All burdens are eventually released.

grandfather of the Wasatch
grandfather of scrub oak and worn mountains

Back in Denmark the family name was everywhere,
the roots of home deeper than marrow.
In Odense, the narrow stone streets and half-timbered cottages
in the old town where you worked and lived,
are markers for your name.

You are the rough man behind the bar serving the locals,
you are the locals being served,
you are the lonesome woman in the corner who is beautiful,
you are your great-grandson
sitting at the bar,
getting to know his great-grandfather.

Learning to Be Human

It's hard to be human
in these bodies that betray us,
with the needfulness of our hearts,
the poverty of our ways,
and our outsized brains that doom us to suffering.

If we are indeed spiritual beings
dwelling in these bodies, learning what we need,
then moving on when time prevails,
let us make these vessels of bone and flesh
homes that feed us as much as we must feed them.

Let us furnish them with
sofas we can sink into without shame,
woodstoves suitable for heating a medium-sized omnivore,
pantries that nourish our varied desires,
and temperance born only of dignity.

Let us use these bodies to school
our trapped souls in temporal matters
of satisfaction and sorrow,
in animal ways of muscle and movement,
in the ecology of our humanness.

Boundless

Sometimes we recognize others as a mirror
that has captured the same light,

a pattern of stories etched on the glass.
A glyph only we can decipher,

understood like the grounding of desert light.
A knowing that my story is your story,

to remind us that we are the same,
that we are strangers but not strangers,

that the universe is big, and we are small,
that all of it is beautiful in its impermanence

and hopeful in its continuation.
That the earth is old, and we are both

young and old together in the turning
where everything is here for us now.

The common and the uncommon,
the miraculous and the banal,

the longing and the allowing
the mark of the hand, the scar on the land.

That all parts are part of all,
not good or bad or indifferent,

not yours or mine, not this piece or that piece,
not this gender or that gender,

not this color or that color,
but the sum of everything.

That unity is our nature,
in this time and that time,

the here and the now,
the why and the how,

the question and the answer,
the dream and the dread, the other instead,

the triumph and the tragedy,
the choice and the consequence,

the anger and the blame,
the acceptance and the shame,

the shout and the silence,
the turning in, the turning out,

the fist and the open hand,
the lion and the lamb,

the final I am,
the umbra and the penumbra.

Together as one, all of us one,
hard as it may be, confounding our fears,

but the circle once broken is an arc,
both ends turning inward to form again.

As River, as Love

Twelve days of solitude
is more than enough time
for a man to know what he loves.

The impossible fold of earth
buckled in embedded layers,
a record of time and tumult.

The way sunlight
attaches itself to the ancient rock,
rendering the storied deposits,

and you,
far downriver and floating west
deep in the red canyon.

I follow the tributaries
of Oak Creek and Pleasant Creek
where mountain waters surge

into desert streams,
then joining the Fremont
whose narrow waters flow

east to the Muddy River
to become the Dirty Devil,
then curving south

to the Colorado
whose chartreuse waters
carry your name,

where at dusk I watch
the weakening light
illuminate the Wingate ramparts

in a red and voluminous glow
then play upon the broad water
from so many rivers

sliding past in great,
glistening fractals,
the spiraling eddies
etched in flat light,
suspended momentarily,
then released downstream

like the flow and interlude of love,
carrying the sum of all we gather,
what we shed and what remains

to make what is real.
The passing of all this sediment
and sentiment through these canyons

cracks open something deep inside,
old and hard as the rock itself
but sinuous like the river,

where under a star-pierced sky,
above the canyon rim
and the vast darkness beyond,

I cast my words of love into the current,
knowing that all my rivers
lead to you.

Garden Manager

Without warning, a dark messenger in the monsoon sky,
wielded his countless icy projectiles
upon the seasonal inhabitants.

Despite the long-necked kale
frantically waving in the wind,
not a plant was spared, they had nowhere to go.

The handsome heirloom romaine permanently disfigured,
the delicate beet greens, pummeled to the earth in a sopping
assault, the ruby-red chard bleeding a thousand tiny deaths.

Even the bolting arugula took a hard hit,
and the languorous squash, with its giant, showy
solar panels, such an easy target.

But there can be no justice for such carnage, nor blame,
there will be no trial, no judgment will be passed.
Yet the sun will arc the following day from the northeast,

another drama on the farm will begin.
The robins will have their way with the worms each dawn,
the garter snakes will slide themselves from the riverbank

each evening to patrol the beds,
the children will chase the ducks back to the pond.
And this tough-love, roll-the-dice venture

will continue, as the cycle of things go,
the yielding and unyielding measures,
the never-nothing dance to stay ahead.

Onward to seed, to the gleaning harvest
and the final surrender to the only
garden manager that really matters.

Fruita Thanksgiving

Breeze enough for comfort,
brushing across the eroded basin,
tires ripping free the pungent mustard fragrance
fusing to the dry, suspended clay.
Spring manifest on this
edge of desert west,
the horizon a dusty red line,
clouds suggesting a sentence
or some cryptic implication of nothing.
Book Cliff single track
crossing and recrossing
the long-dry drainages
dotted with splattered bovine pies
drying in the sun.
Past a newly dead calf
with half-eaten rump
and missing eyes,
the flies having their way.
Turkey vultures
arcing the blue above,
dragonflies trailing their iridescent fuselages,
every creature doing its job.
Impossible to feel important, being human,
or to wonder at small misfortunes,
with this spread of wild and ravaged land.
Death and life in all its churning and buzzing splendor,
a good home down the road
anchored to the old earth and pointing to the winter sun,
a beaver in the pond
stealing away one cottonwood at a time
under a sky riddled with stars.

Morning light in the guest-bedroom window,
cracked open to receive a cacophony of birds.
Feeling full with books on the shelf,
coffee on the stove
and a friend at the kitchen counter,
grinning like he should be.

Amity

for Carolina

traveler
enter
your weariness here
shall not bear alone

wayfarer
closer
your shoulder here
need not carry the stone

friend
sit
acceptance here
has shaped you a home

Andean Ascents, a Love Story

You are tired again.
Your third trip south from Quito
beyond the low-lying tendrils of the sprawling city,
past the cultivated mountainsides shrouded in cloud
toward your fourth and final volcano.

At 15,000 feet, you arrive at your third hut in seven days.
You will claim your bunk and thin mattress
mumble greetings to fellow climbers
sort and lay out your gear
and start assembling your temporary edifice
to guard a few hours of precious sleep.

You will get little and the tyranny of the clock
will catch you soon enough.
Like a man to the gallows,
you head to the dining room
for breakfast at 11:00 p.m.
amid several languages you do not know.
You are aware you signed up for the surreal
night climb to come.

As your team gathers you confirm your
readiness as the headlamps come on
and the clamber of heavy boots
echoes off the hardwood floor.
You feel strong and determined
but a nagging doubt will hitch a ride
on your pack taunting you with her cruel refrain:

Hombre, do you have what it takes;
perhaps your best years are behind you.

You shrug her off and bang out the first hour
without thought, gaining 600 feet.
At 16,000 feet you force the truth of your frailty aside
your only job now is to keep up with the team.
You'll get to stop every hour for five minutes
but only if you ask, revealing your weakness.
Keep it short, time is not your friend
and the mountain is waiting above to kill you.

At 17,000 feet your team puts on their crampons
and pulls out their ice axes.
The tongue of the glacier looms above you.
You rope up and climb onto her buckled back
you feel the bite of your crampons
the stick-thud rhythm of your axe.
Here you must make every step count
be ready to arrest but not too ready.
Your axe is a tether connecting you to the
ever-shifting glacier beneath your feet.

Hombre, why have you left your family
for the cold mountain; she will only betray you.

Resist looking at your watch
you have not gained much more elevation.
Resist trying to see the perils around you:
avalanche from recent snows, slope disappearing
into blackness, building-sized seracs ready to topple above
crevasses below, sure icy death if you fall and cannot arrest.
Your family, your lover, your pet,
none will forgive your selfishness.

Try not to imagine your falling body
tearing itself apart on the moraine.
Try not to accept that you are too tired to care.
stick/step/breath, stick/step/breath,
do this a thousand times and you are nowhere
follow the rope and give it your life.

*Hombre, you are a fool, nobody cares you
are up here, especially the mountain;
only a few will care if you come down.*

Like a terrible dream, the line between
one world and another blurs as the hours
peel away and fall into the void.
A looming mass will appear above you
that is the steaming beast you are riding
humble yourself and ask for safe passage.

At 18,000 feet, know that the middle gain is the hardest.
This is the wilderness of your long night,
it does have an edge, but you may not find it.
Keep your head down and follow the track ahead.
You will want to quit but nobody will have
empathy for you, especially yourself.

Hombre, perhaps you have not trained hard enough.

This is when you must love yourself the most.
Be kind as the mountain may not be.
When the sky begins to illuminate itself
you will realize only 1,000 feet
separates you from the summit.
You can see a new day being born above the massif
this is the light you should follow.

Strive to divide this number by half
dig deeper into the spleen of yourself.
This is all that matters now, you and the mountain
the dome of heaven brightening above.
You have sacrificed everything to be here,
months of training, your accounts drained,
your work pushed aside, loved ones distanced.

Hombre, you have a chance
of summiting, but still you may fail.

At 19,000 feet you have fully inhabited your suffering.
The beauty of the mountain is part of you now
its rugged grandeur is burned into your eyes
its contours are recorded in your bones.
You cannot imagine being anywhere else
nothing can stop you.
Stick/step/breath, stick/step/breath,
do not forget you are on the holy flank of the world.

Keep going until abruptly
there is nowhere left to climb.
But take the last few steps to the summit slowly.
Find the highest ground and claim your rapture
sending it out to the playa below.
Feel the strength you have somehow gathered,
take in the view you have earned.
This is why you are here.
It is both everything and nothing at all.

What I Know So Far

That the heart
is wiser than the head,
that equanimity
is harder than partiality.

dawn arrives
new sun rends the silence
clouds gather
dryland farmer waits for rain

That the better part of us
is connection,
that all boxes
are empty boxes.

flicker hammers
the snag yields
elk bugles
the hunter advances

That terror and grace
reside together,
that this time around,
we are the asteroid.

fall turns
the wood man comes in his truck
winter pulls in
birds lift from the snow

That love can become
a form of trading,
that science
is a story.

the heart roars
the mind stills
the hand closes
the hollow forms

Notes

Manuscript editing by Lynda La Rocca.

"Come Back to Us Everett Ruess"
Everett Ruess (March 28, 1914–c. November 1934) was an American artist, poet, and writer. He carried out solo explorations of the High Sierras, the California coast, and most notably, the high desert regions of the Colorado Plateau. In 1934, at age 20, he disappeared while traveling through a remote area of Southern Utah; his fate remains one of the enduring mysteries of the Southwest.

The author of this collection has made two trips to Davis Gulch in south-central Utah, Ruess's last known location, to search for clues relating to his disappearance.

"Missing Climber on Mount Harvard"
Around September 21, 2013, Gene George, a 64-year-old attorney and seasonal "peak bagger" from Cleveland, Ohio, went missing somewhere on the Mount Harvard massif in the central Rockies of Colorado. Search efforts at the time involved more than 100 volunteers from seven counties, along with three helicopters, one fixed-wing aircraft, several dog teams, two horseback teams, two mules, and numerous items of specialized equipment. Efforts to find George were suspended after four days of searching.

The author of this collection was climbing Mount Harvard and the adjacent Mount Columbia at the same time George was on the mountain. He discovered a note left by George on the summit of Mount Columbia which was reported to the county sheriff's department and later retrieved by helicopter to aid in the search. Six months later Gene George's wallet and articles of clothing were found by a hiker lower in the basin, which led to the discovery of his remains on March 24, 2014.

About the Author

Craig Nielson is a poet, architect, climber, and explorer of desert landscapes. He writes, designs, climbs, and explores from his home base in the central Rockies of Colorado. He is the founding member of the Southern-Colorado-based performance-poetry troupe River City Nomads and co-organizer of the quarterly live poetry event "Season of Words" in Salida, Colorado

His first collection of poems, *Touch of Grace,* was published by Ghost Road Press in 2005. His work has appeared in *Pilgrimage, Mountain Gazette,* and *Colorado Central Magazine,* along with the anthologies *A Democracy of Poets, Open Windows 2005,* and *Telling It Real,* and the chapbook, *On Stage: River City Nomads.*

www.ingramcontent.com/pod-product-compliance
Lightning Source LLC
Chambersburg PA
CBHW022146160426
43197CB00009B/1454